The Grassington to East Coast Walk

written & researched

by

John White

Fractal Press

Chapters

Photographs

Large Scale Maps

Cover by BoE Designs.

Reproduced by permission of Ordnance Survey
on behalf of The Controller of Her Majesty's
Stationery Office © Crown Copyright. License
Number: 100040928

British Library Cataloguing in Publication Data
A catalogue record of this book is available from
the British Library

ISBN 1 870735 30 7

GRASSINGTON

TWINNED WITH DODGE CITY

Welcome to Grassington

Introduction

*T*he 100 miles of this new walk between Grassington and Robin Hood's Bay goes through splendid countryside, quite a lot of which lies between the Yorkshire Dales National Park and the North Yorkshire Moors National Park.

National Parks have protected some of the most beautiful country that we have but the impression is that anything outside their boundaries must have something wrong with it. This is not true of Nidderdale or the Fountains Earth Moors to Masham. Nor is it true of the Vale of Mowbray, where easy walking crosses good country down ancient lanes and pleasant footpaths.

Although this walk is intended to be a fine, relaxing, holiday it does require some effort. However, instead of pushing yourself to the limit I suggest that you have a break and enjoy a pleasant tramp from here to the coast. There is no doubt that at the end of every day you will be a little footsore, healthily exercised and looking forward to good food and the odd drink. In the unpredictable weather of our country the character of the walk can change dramatically from quite easy in fine weather to quite difficult if the ground is wet and slippery. On the tops, snow can add an extra touch of pleasure but we don't seem to get much of that these days.

The route is neither arduous nor dull but a pleasure for walkers of any age or experience who want to spend a week in fresh air during the day and in a comfortable bed each night. The idea is to travel light and stay in the pubs and guesthouses that are available along the way but there are no rules, do what you prefer or can afford.

I have had many wonderful days exploring each section of the route. I did not think there could be a better walking experience until, in the company of five friends from Grassington, we made our way along the whole route for the first time.

We all live in Wharfedale, so our first day was the longest. Rather than stopping in Nidderdale, we decided to do the first two days of the walk in one. So we struck off up the hill to Yarnbury, then beyond, over heather and moor to Middlesmoor for lunch, before setting out again for the distant town of Masham. It is thirty miles by road to Masham, but 'only' twenty one by the route we took (the route in this book it is now a bit further - continental drift, I think). Unless you are familiar with the area, I recommend that you take your time and do each section as described in the following pages. You may only pass this way once, so you may as well enjoy the journey.

The Grassington to East Coast Walk is not a 'natural' route walked for centuries by monks or packhorses, in fact, until October 2000 it had never been walked from end to end. Then it was that a scary group gathered, bleary eyed and without any dress sense, to look at the sky, eat butties and try to make conversation. None of us had done seven consecutive days of walking before but we now found ourselves committed and with no way out. We had it all to do and no certainty that we could do it.

Eventually, we took commemorative photographs - Ray Davey, Richard Foster, Dave Heseltine, Rob Keep, Paul Kent, John White and Perry, who accompanied us on the first day. Then we turned our backs on the cobbles of Grassington Square to head up hill accompanied by the rustle of windproofs and the tinkle of fridge magnets falling off Perry's economy size rucksack.

I hope you enjoy it as much as we did.

Day One

Terrain: Walled fields and open moor
Exposed and away from all human habitation
Distance: 12 miles
Total height gain: 1930 ft
Maximum elevation: 1788 ft (at Sandy Gate)
Constant Walking Time: 4 - 5 hours
Refreshment: Packed lunch
Allow 6 hours

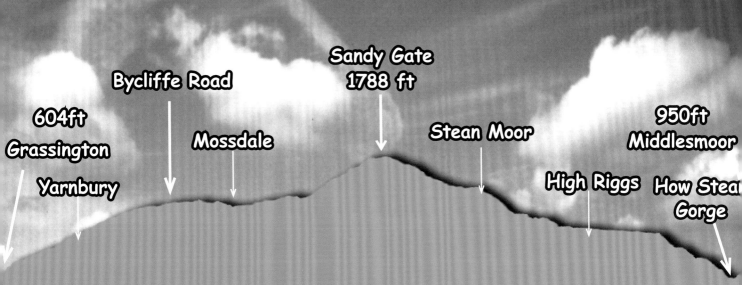

Sandy Gate
1788 ft

Bycliffe Road

604ft
Grassington

Mossdale

Stean Moor

950ft
Middlesmoor

Yarnbury

High Riggs

How Stean
Gorge

Grassington to Nidderdale

*T*his is a great day to set off on the Grassington to East Coast Walk, and what a day! A day to remember. One hundred miles to do, and every single one offering good views (never cloudy or misty), fine weather (it never rains), and free beer in all the pubs.

On this first day, you will climb to the highest point on the whole walk at 1788ft. This is in the middle of a vast open moor at the watershed between Wharfedale and Nidderdale. It may be of interest to reflect that when you are at Mossdale Scar the nearest road behind you is three and a half miles away. South to Greenhow the road is six miles away. And to the north, round the other side of Great Whernside, it is three miles to the road into Coverdale. Ahead another five miles to Nidderdale's roads. Altogether you will be in the middle of a moor that amounts to over 130 square miles of land. Don't let it worry you – no-one has ever been lost up here for more than five days.

One of the novelties of the first two days of this walk is that once you are through Mossdale and onto Stean Moor you are walking down the eastern slopes of the Pennine hills. Between you and the North Yorkshire Moors (30 miles away as the crow flies) is the Vale of Mowbray, hidden in the dip, so you can see across those miles to a line of hills where, with a bit of effort, you will be in two or three days time. On a sharp clear day look south east for the White Horse carved into the hillside many miles away at Kilburn. It shines out in the sun.

Once in Nidderdale it is worth an hour or two of your time to visit the dramatic How Stean Gorge (especially after heavy rain). There is a cafe for a snack after you have walked down into the gullies next to the deep flowing stream, crossed the little wooden bridges and stumbled through the friendly pot hole.

The following pages describe the route for each day in some detail. The description breaks the walk up into a number of sections between 'waypoints' which are usually placed at natural turnings or important places. I have not mentioned every stile or field that has to be crossed. Instead, I have included the best Ordnance Survey maps - 1:25000 (2¹/₂ inches to the mile) which show every track and all field boundaries. The best advise for following the guide without getting lost is to trust the map first and use the instructions to make sure you are going the right way. The arrows on the map show the recommended route for each day, with different coloured arrows where there are interesting alternatives. The Waypoint numbers also appear on the map as small coloured rectangles with the number in white - e.g. WP22 WP22 WP22 so you can identify the nearest waypoint from the map and then follow the directions in the text as well as the arrows. The distance to the next waypoint should help you to pace your walk for the greatest comfort as well as knowing when to anticipate a turn.

The altitude data, on the first page of each chapter was generated from GPS data and is intended to help you anticipate the effort that will be required each day. Don't be put off by the altitude graphs, they are exaggerated to produce a profile of hills, they are not mountains, the highest is 1800 ft - if it was produced to scale across 100 miles it would be little more than a flat line!

Map 1. Grassington to Bycliffe Road with Alternative Route through Grasswood & Conistone Dib

Bare House

See detailed map & directions p.18

Day 1. Grassington to Upper Nidderdale

WP01
1.5 miles
NNE to WP02

With the Devonshire Hotel on your left, the first steps of the Grassington to East Coast Walk lead up hill out of the left hand side of Grassington Square. Continue up past the Foresters Arms, (on the right) some shops, the library, a crossroad and the Octagon Theatre (on your right). Soon you will be out of the village, climbing steeply up the road that leads all the way to Yarnbury. Map 1, Page 12 (M1,p12).

WP02
0.75 miles
N to WP03

At Yarnbury, 20 yards beyond the entrance to the house, turn left along a bridleway with fingerpost and follow a winding track between two walls. Eventually High Barn & Bare House will be visible a hundred yards away from the path to your left. M1,p12.

Buttercup Meadow

Mossdale

WP03
0.35 mile
N to WP04

The path continues over pleasant springy ground to a fingerpost. M1,p.12.

WP04
0.8 miles
N to WP05

At the finger post to Gill House on the right. Keep to the track on the left all the way to Bycliffe Road. M1/2, p.12/15.

WP05
1 mile
NE to WP06

Turn right and follow the track down into Mossdale. Mossdale Scar is round the first corner. M2, p.15.

WP06
0.35 miles
NE to WP07

A substantial stone shooting house just beyond the scar is on the other side of the stream. M2.p.15.

WP07
1 mile
NE to WP08

Next to the shooting house, a finger post points up onto the moor, along a sheep trod. It is a gentle slope up to a small stone shelter. 1 Negotiate a little bit of bog to get to the highest point on the whole East Coast Walk, at 1788 ft. M2,p.15.

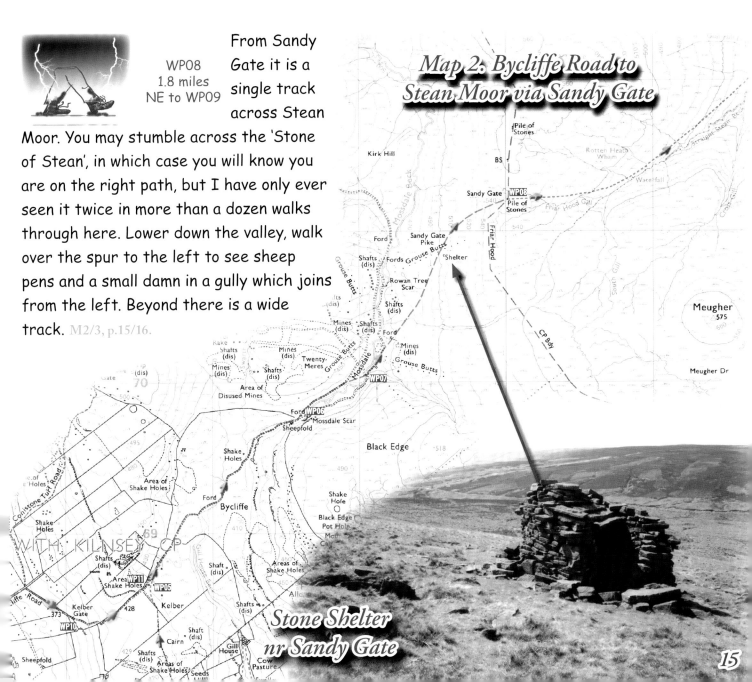

WP08
1.8 miles
NE to WP09

From Sandy Gate it is a single track across Stean Moor. You may stumble across the 'Stone of Stean', in which case you will know you are on the right path, but I have only ever seen it twice in more than a dozen walks through here. Lower down the valley, walk over the spur to the left to see sheep pens and a small damn in a gully which joins from the left. Beyond there is a wide track. M2/3, p.15/16.

Map 2: Bycliffe Road to Stean Moor via Sandy Gate

Stone Shelter nr Sandy Gate

WP09
1.6 miles
NE to WP10

Follow the wide track for over a mile to a gate, on the other side of which turn right towards a tumble-down barn on the right of the track leading to High Riggs Farm. M3,p.16.

WP10
0.8 miles
E to WP11

Walk down hill through High Riggs Farm and beyond through two lush meadows that drop quickly down the spur to How Stean Beck. Over the stream coming in from the left the path begins to climb up again on the left. M3,p.16.

WP11
0.4 miles
SE to WP12

A stile on the left at the top of the incline leads through two fields to the village of Middlesmoor at WP12. M3,p16.

Day 1. Alternative to How Stean Gorge & Lofthouse. Map 3, page 16.

WP01
0.5 miles
SE to WP02

At the style **WP11**, now WP01 of the alternative route, continue down the path for half a mile, through the trees with the top end of the gorge on your right.

WP02
150 yards
SW to WP03

Turn right to cross a footbridge and a good view into part of the gorge. Up the other side to the road through a small field with a single caravan in it.

WP03
0.5 miles
SE to WP04

Turn left and walk down the road for half a mile towards WP04 but the entrance to the gorge, with cafe and peacocks is only half that distance. Don't forget the pleasant little pothole, it's for kids of all ages. After your visit, turn left out of the gate and continue to the bridge.

WP04
0.25 miles
NE to WP05

Turn left and join the bigger road at a left hand bend. Ahead on the right hand bend in a lay-by turn left again to take you up the fields to Middlesmoor, or follow the road round to Lofthouse.

Stone on Stean Moor

How Stean

Day 1. Grass Wood & Conistone Dib Alternative

Map 4 page 18, detail to Grass Wood. Main Map page 12.

 WP01
0.2 miles
NNW to WP02
If you haven't been to either Grass Wood or Conistone Dib this alternative route is well worth considering. It adds a couple of miles to the first day, so you have to assess your fitness. At the crossroads (WP01) turn left into Chapel Lane. Continue to a finger post on the right.

 WP02
0.2 miles
NW to WP03
Turn right up Bank Laithe, a finger post shows the Dales Way, Kettlewell in the same direction. Walk to a sharp right hand bend just after a double stable on the right, and a metal farm gate in front.

 WP03
0.25 miles
NW to WP04
Turn left into a field, before the farm gate, across a little footbridge (a plank), to a stile in the wall opposite. Then turn half left, over another wall and then, crossing a path that runs north, go to a stile over a third wall. The field on the other side drops down hill and the path curves round to the bottom corner where a stile gives access to Cove Lane at WP04. Grass Wood can be seen across the field on the right.

WP04
250 yards
N to WP05
Walk ahead with a barn on your right to the end of the walled lane and then, through a gate, turn half right to cross a field near to another barn, and the stile into Grass Wood is ahead . Map 1 Page 12 from here.

WP05
0.5 miles
NW to WP06
Strike away from the edge of the wood gently up hill into the trees, and continue on this path to a four way finger post. Turn left to visit Fort Gregory, a beautiful castellated medieval fortification with drawbridge, spiral staircases and deep dungeons? Sorry, no, just a pile of stones.

WP06
0.5 miles
NE to WP07
From the four way fingerpost turn right, the way leads over a stile into Bastow Wood, a slightly thinner woodland with the limestone showing through in

Map 4. Grassington to Grasswood detail.

18

Wharfedale Sunset

places, the path winding slightly, until it emerges from the trees with an old empty dew pond on the left and a wall with a stile directly in front.

 WP07
125 yards
N to WP08
Turn left, in front of you are up-ended limestone scars. Cross the stile, and drop down steeply into a little gully and then climb up the other side. The stile is built into the wall in the left hand corner. Cross the stile. Down to the left is the top end of a deep enclosed box canyon. Turn left and follow the path next to the wall until it turns more northerly over the end of the scars, through a gate and down two or three fields into the village of Conistone.

 WP08
1.25 miles
NE to WP09
In the middle of Conistone at WP08 turn right off the road and up to a five bar gate which leads to a second gate immediately, and then round the corner to the beginnings of Conistone Dib. Follow it through an amazing feature, it levels out and then half way up crosses a wall over a stile that is slightly off to the left, then on up into the narrowing corner of the feature with a little climb out at the top.

Map 2, page 15 from here.

 WP09
0.7 miles
NE to WP10
At the top, cross the stile, turn left and go through the gate. There is a finger post pointing right to Middlesmoor 8 miles. Turn right and follow the track up through another gate and then to a right hand turn and the next gate, Kelber Gate, is WP10.

 WP10
0.35 miles
NE to WP11
Follow the track round and rejoin the main route at WP11/WP05.

GRASSINGTON 12M

EAST COAST 88M

Day Two

Terrain: Open moor, wide and easy, mostly downhill
Distance: 15 miles
Total height gain: 780 ft
Highest point: 1372 ft
Constant walking time: 5 hours
Refreshment: late lunch in Masham
Allow 7 hours

Middlesmoor
950 ft

Shooting House
1300 ft

Fountains Earth

Jenny Twigg
& her
daughter Tib

Ilton

Masham

Snape
&
Thorp Perrow

Gebdykes

Upper Nidderdale to Snape

This day's walk is a treat on legs. It starts with a swift, steep climb gaining height that is not lost again for over six miles. These are lofty miles high above the surrounding landscape with long distance views on all sides. It is a time to float along, head held high to get it up and into the clouds. Walk with your head in the clouds today and you will carry the exhilaration with you for many more days to come.

It is a spectacular day for this 'short' walk to Masham for lunch and then Snape, and it can be so different from one day to the next, depending on the weather you bring with you. You have to book the weather that you want on the internet when you book your accommodation. Here are your choices:

On a sunny day there is no better place and the distance just falls away as you fly across the open moors that are collectively known as Fountains Earth.

On a breezy day with broken cloud, the sun comes and goes like a shutter opening and closing in a skylight.

On the dark heath, low cloud subdues the colours into reddish browns and stony greys. There are mysterious monoliths stalking the moor to your right – *Jenny Twigg and her Daughter Tib* – looking quite dangerous in the gloom, keep an eye on them in case they move.

High winds from the east make this moor into a real adventure. The Gales sneak onto the land off the North Sea through a low gap in the hills and blast their way across the Vale below and up the Pennine hills, full of sharp chills that will burn your face into a rosy glow by evening.

These lofty miles of today's walk are all about the sky, it is so big and close, you can touch it on grey days and even breathe it when it really closes in. However, a strange phenomenon of high vantage points is that you can often see through the gap between ground and cloud to sun lit fields up ahead. Keep walking, the sun is chasing across the landscape towards you.

Beyond Masham, at Five Lane Ends there is the lovely Moor Lane, which is a joy to walk along. Not only quiet, easy and gently down hill, but offering a raised view across the Vale of Mowbray which is now laid out below.

It is only 11 miles to Masham from Middlesmoor, so you should aim to get to Masham for lunch, or at least late lunch. This should give you a couple of hours to look round before completing the remaining four and a half miles to Snape for a pleasant stay in the comfortable Castle Arms Inn.

Upper Nidderdale

The Shooting House is up here

Day 2. Middlesmoor to Snape

WP01
300 yards
E to WP02

From Middlesmoor walk across the road between the houses on the corner opposite the pub. Through a five bar gate and over a stile on the right. Map 5, page 24.

WP02
0.75 miles
NE to WP03

Drop diagonally down hill across the field making for a gap in the narrow wood ahead and continue beyond it to the road. Cross the road, over (a very small stile) into the field as far as the stream. Turn left. M5,p.24.

Map 5. Middlesmoor to Fountains Earth

WP03
300 yards
N to WP04

At the little bridge below Thrope Farm turn right and walk up round the back of the buildings. M5,p.24.

WP04
0.25 miles
E to WP05

In the farm yard turn left through a five bar gate and head straight up the middle of the field, the hillside is steep for 400 yards. Through a gate and half left, steeply up hill. M5,p.24.

WP05
0.25 miles
NE to WP06

The path turns left and continues slightly less steeply and on a pleasant path upwards eventually arriving at a five bar gate onto the moor and only a hundred yards from the impressive shooting house that commands a wonderful view across the valley. M5,p.24.

Map 6. Fountains Earth to Ilton

WP06
300 yards
S to WP07

The track runs behind the Shooting House to the right, wide and clear. M5,p.24.

WP07
0.4 miles
SE to WP08

At the left hand bend, follow it round with a wall on your right for less than half a mile to a road. M5,p.24.

WP08
150 yards
NE to WP09

Turn left up the road for 150 yards. M5,p.24.

WP09
0.5 miles
SE to WP10

Turn right onto a wide bridleway. Follow this wide, lofty track for over four glorious miles across several moors that are collectively known as Fountains Earth because it was all once controlled by Fountains Abbey. Keep left at the first junction. M5,p.24.

Across Fountains Earth, Cleveland Ridge in the distance

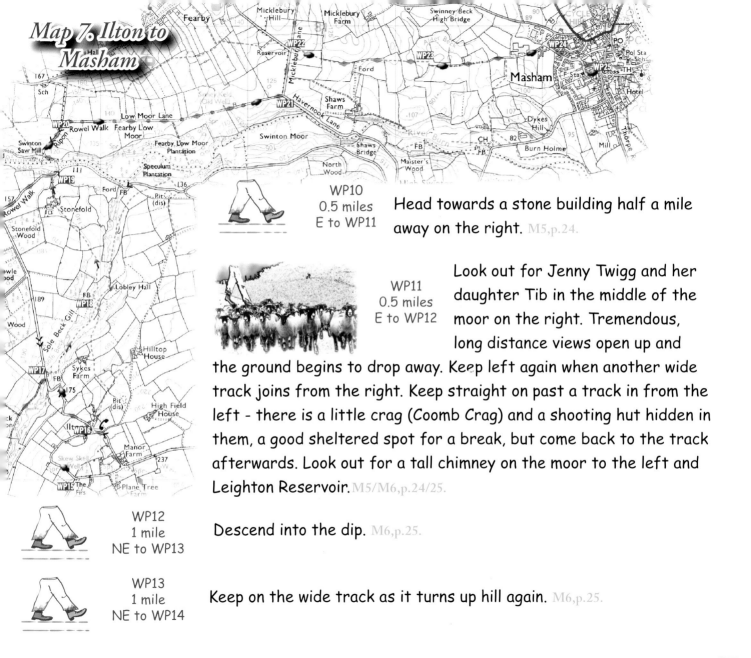

Map 7. Ilton to Masham

WP10
0.5 miles
E to WP11

Head towards a stone building half a mile away on the right. M5,p.24.

WP11
0.5 miles
E to WP12

Look out for Jenny Twigg and her daughter Tib in the middle of the moor on the right. Tremendous, long distance views open up and the ground begins to drop away. Keep left again when another wide track joins from the right. Keep straight on past a track in from the left - there is a little crag (Coomb Crag) and a shooting hut hidden in them, a good sheltered spot for a break, but come back to the track afterwards. Look out for a tall chimney on the moor to the left and Leighton Reservoir. M5/M6,p.24/25.

WP12
1 mile
NE to WP13

Descend into the dip. M6,p.25.

WP13
1 mile
NE to WP14

Keep on the wide track as it turns up hill again. M6,p.25.

**WP14
1.4 miles
NE to WP15**
This is the most important turn of the day, left, with a bank of rocks on the right, the track dips downhill just shy of the ridge. A large plantation is half a mile ahead on the left. Through a gate, up ahead the track surface becomes tarmac. The moors are left behind. Walk to the junction. M6,p.25.

**WP15
0.25 miles
NE to WP16**
Turn left, the road circles round to the collection of houses called Ilton. M7,p.27.

**WP16
0.40 miles
NW to WP17**
At the junction turn left again and follow the road down the steep hill. At the bottom there is a footbridge on the left for when the stream floods over the road and there is a barn on the right. M7,p.27.

**WP17
0.4 miles
SW to WP18**
Turn right behind the

barn, recross the stream (Sole Beck) and walk down the little valley with the stream on your left, until you cross to your left. M7,p.27.

 WP18
0.6 miles
NW to WP19 Walk over the rise through fields, through Stonefold Farm and onto the road over the stile. M7,p.27.

 **WP19**
0.2 miles
NE to WP20 Cross the road and walk down to and over the road bridge in the trees, round two bends, slightly up hill, until, on your right, you will see a mosaic for the Ripon Rowel Walk. It is at the beginning of Low Moor Lane. Turn right. M7,p.27.

 **WP20**
1 mile
E to WP21 Follow Low Moor Lane to the junction at the end. Turn left. M7,p.27.

A bit of weather

WP21
0.25 miles
N to WP22

Turn left, pass the first footpath sign on the right, and walk to the corner at the top, where the tarmac road bends left, the track continues without tarmac and the footpath is on the right marked by a tall post. M7,p.27.

WP22
0.7 miles
E to WP23

Follow the path through fields to a large barn. M7,p.27.

WP23
0.5 miles
NE to WP24

The path heads slightly north of east and eventually becomes a road between buildings. Take the first turn on the right. M7,p.27.

Lunch

WP24
0.3 miles
E to WP25

Turn right and wind through the streets to find the open square in the centre of Masham. M7,p.27.

This is quite a late lunch, after a steady walk. You should relax and take a break - visit the brewery, perhaps. Although there are another four and half miles to Snape, you can consider yourself to be out of the Dales and onto the Vale of Mowbray. There is a low ridge to climb up to Gebdykes Farm, but the going is now easy and mostly down hill. It should take little more than an hour and a half, so use the time to have a good look round Masham.

John White

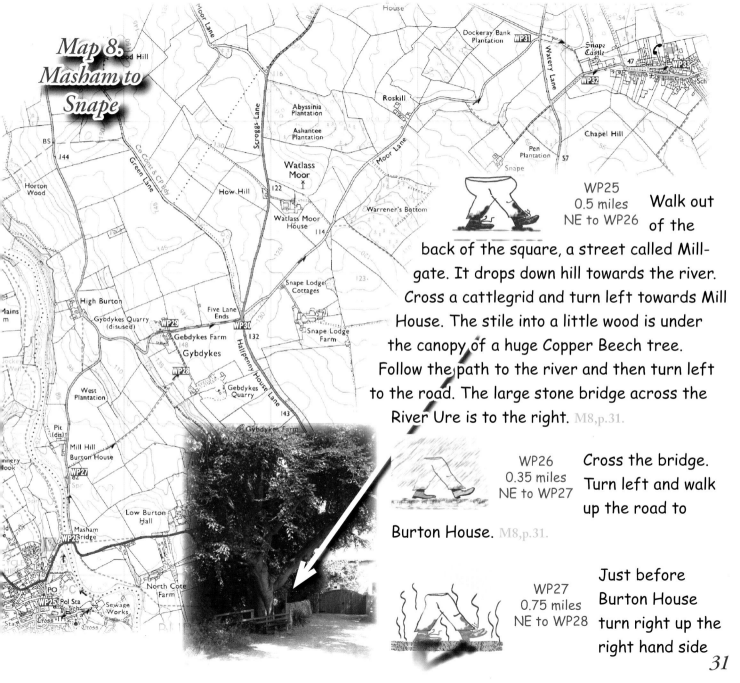

Map 8: Masham to Snape

WP25
0.5 miles
NE to WP26

Walk out of the back of the square, a street called Mill-gate. It drops down hill towards the river. Cross a cattlegrid and turn left towards Mill House. The stile into a little wood is under the canopy of a huge Copper Beech tree. Follow the path to the river and then turn left to the road. The large stone bridge across the River Ure is to the right. M8,p.31.

WP26
0.35 miles
NE to WP27

Cross the bridge. Turn left and walk up the road to Burton House. M8,p.31.

WP27
0.75 miles
NE to WP28

Just before Burton House turn right up the right hand side

of a field. The path is straight on up the left hand side of the next field and then disappears into the left hand corner where a stile helps you over the fence. It is straight up hill to the corner of the next fence that you will see on the close horizon, then half left to a stile on to the track. M8,p.31.

WP28
250 yards
N to WP29

Turn left, the wide track leads to Gebdykes Farm.
M8,p.31.

WP29
0.4 miles
E to WP30

Turn right onto a fine mature avenue to Five Lane Ends. M8,p.31.

WP30
2 miles
NE to WP31

At the aptly named Five Lanes Ends go straight across onto Moor Lane, relax and enjoy a pleasant two mile interlude gently strolling with open views across the Vale of Mowbray and blue remembered hills in the distance. M8,p.31.

Moor Lane towards Snape

Snape Castle

WP31
0.25 miles
SE to WP32

At Watery Lane, the stile to Snape is opposite across the road. It leads into a field and to the back of Snape Castle. M8,p.31.

WP32
0.75 miles
E to WP33

When you come out onto the road in Snape, turn left, and a short distance further on, there is a farm yard which gives free access to the parts of the castle that are open to the public. Snape has a good pub, The Castle Arms, it provides a friendly atmosphere, nine secluded and quiet double rooms, as well as very good food and a pleasant pint. M8,p.31.

GRASSINGTON 27M

EAST COAST 73M

Day Three

Terrain: Country lanes, tracks, & field paths
Distance: 14 miles
Height Gain: 50 ft
Maximum Height 110 ft
Constant walking time: 5 hours
Allow 6 hours
Refreshments: Bedale & Scruton

Snape
Firby
Bedale
Scruton
Morton-on-Swale
Maunby
South Otterington

Snape to
South Otterington

*T*his is an amazing day's walk. Relax,
enjoy the easy terrain, country lanes, the
little market town of Bedale, numerous villages, a splendid pub
for lunch, and the genuine feeling of making steady progress across a huge
landscape. North of Snape is the mature land that has been given over to trees, and it
shows in the old oaks and beeches that provide shelter and accommodation for birds
and squirrels.

Not only quiet and easy terrain, but pastoral views, like an old sepia
photograph of labour intensive farming, sanitized as healthy
exercise on warm and sunny days. This land is full of trees.
Round each corner on these lower parts of the Vale of
Mowbray look for glimpses of distant views, and although
the hills we are walking towards can often be seen, they
are invariably framed by trees, a million of which are
scattered across the landscape. They are in the

middle of
fields, not
sacrificed to the
convenience of the harvester. Little
groves break up a fierce wind when it sweeps in
from the north. If you have the bonus of a pleasant gale the
trees roar with appreciation and dance and wave their arms, as we should
too. There are many interesting trees to be seen in the Arboretum, Thorp
Perrow, on the northern edge of Snape. There you will find collections that
were first planted in the 1840s. They include Oak, Chinese Maples, an
avenue of Limes, Walnut, Beech and a large collection of Pine trees
from around the world.

Trees always frame a great sky, but there are some landscapes
that need no frame. Beyond the bustle of the pretty town of
Bedale, south of Morton-on-Swale, the flat lands next to
the river, lose trees, lose hedges, fences, the lot, and leave
the eye to gaze on a huge sky, a blue dome across our
head from horizon to horizon.

Day 3. Snape to South Otterington

WP01
0.3 miles
N to WP02

The footpath from the Castle Arms in Snape is up the left hand side of the pub, a straight track to a right hand corner. M9,p38. ➔

WP02
0.2 miles
E to WP03

Turn right across open fields until you reach another footpath that crosses from right to left. There is a house a couple of hundred yards over the field on the left. Turn left towards the trees along the new track. In the narrow wood, cross a wooden platform and bear slightly right to find a five bar gate with yellow marker on it. M9,p38.

WP03
0.4 miles
NNWto WP04

Through the gate into open pasture, with well spaced mature trees.

At the far end walk between two cottages and then out onto the back road into Thorp Perrow. Turn right. M9,p38.

WP04
0.25 miles
NE to WP05

Walk north to the little hamlet of Firby.
M9,p38.

Bedale

WP05
1 mile
N to WP06

Map 9.
Snape to
Bedale

Either walk up the quiet lane to Bedale, or after the last house on the right find the fieldpath that curls round from north east to north and then to north west. Bedale is a good place for morning coffee, and a stroll round the picturesque main street. To avail ourselves of a safe crossing over the A1 we head north on a quiet road to the village of Scruton. M9,p38.

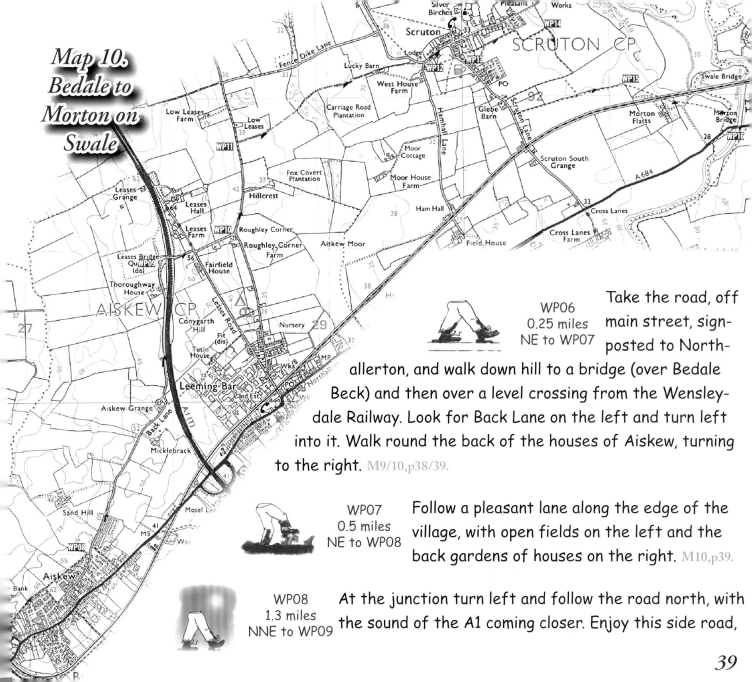

Map 10.
Bedale to
Morton on
Swale

WP06
0.25 miles
NE to WP07

Take the road, off main street, signposted to North-allerton, and walk down hill to a bridge (over Bedale Beck) and then over a level crossing from the Wensley-dale Railway. Look for Back Lane on the left and turn left into it. Walk round the back of the houses of Aiskew, turning to the right. M9/10,p38/39.

WP07
0.5 miles
NE to WP08

Follow a pleasant lane along the edge of the village, with open fields on the left and the back gardens of houses on the right. M10,p39.

WP08
1.3 miles
NNE to WP09

At the junction turn left and follow the road north, with the sound of the A1 coming closer. Enjoy this side road,

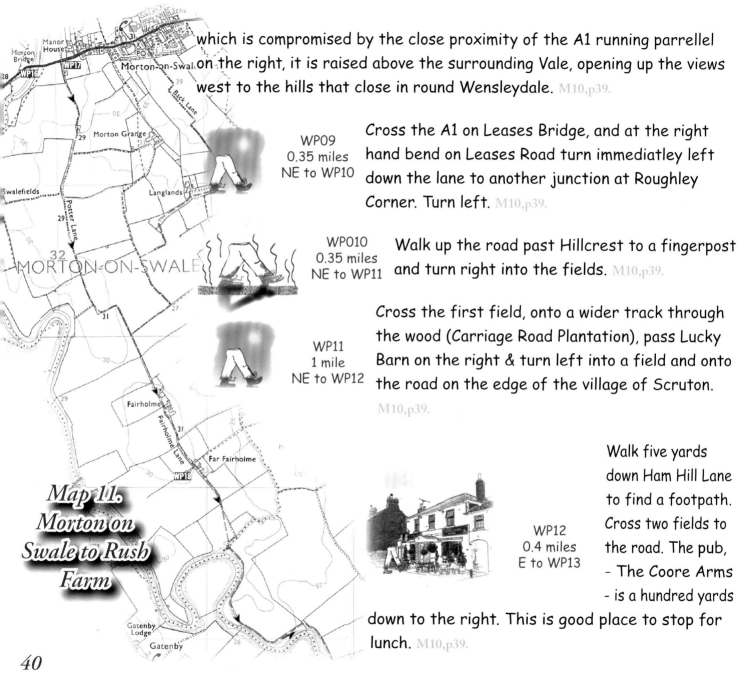

which is compromised by the close proximity of the A1 running parrellel on the right, it is raised above the surrounding Vale, opening up the views west to the hills that close in round Wensleydale. M10,p39.

WP09
0.35 miles
NE to WP10

Cross the A1 on Leases Bridge, and at the right hand bend on Leases Road turn immediatley left down the lane to another junction at Roughley Corner. Turn left. M10,p39.

WP010
0.35 miles
NE to WP11

Walk up the road past Hillcrest to a fingerpost and turn right into the fields. M10,p39.

WP11
1 mile
NE to WP12

Cross the first field, onto a wider track through the wood (Carriage Road Plantation), pass Lucky Barn on the right & turn left into a field and onto the road on the edge of the village of Scruton. M10,p39.

Map 11.
Morton on
Swale to Rush
Farm

WP12
0.4 miles
E to WP13

Walk five yards down Ham Hill Lane to find a footpath. Cross two fields to the road. The pub, - The Coore Arms - is a hundred yards down to the right. This is good place to stop for lunch. M10,p39.

WP13
0.3 miles
NE to WP14

After lunch turn right out of the
pub back up towards the village, the
path turns right behind the top row of
houses but you can link into it again a few hundred yards east if you want to walk through the
rest of the village. M10,p39.

WP14
0.4 miles
SE to WP15

The path turns south, jinks right (west) then south again before
turning east to the end of the field. Turn half right to a gate,
a short paddock away from the railway line and Morton Farm (the
stile is inside the hawthorn hedge). M10,p39.

WP15
0.35 miles
SE to WP16

A large ladder stile can be seen diagonally across the paddock, it leads
up to the railway line. Cross the line (not in use at the time of writ-
ing but eventually going to re-open, so take a little care) and turn left,
the way out is very well concealed under dark bushes about ten yards away. Climb over the stile

into the field and walk half left towards the gates next to the farm road. The path continues through the gate at an angle across the next field towards Morton Bridge which can be seen from here. M10,p39.

WP16
200 yards
E to WP17

Cross the bridge but pass by the first footpath on the right - it winds along the river bank (if you want to follow the river for a while it joins Potter Lane at Swalefields). A hundred yards beyond the river side path is a wide tarmac bridleway, turn south. M11,p40.

The River Swale at Maunby

WP17
1.8 miles
S to WP18
Follow the pleasant 'flatlands' bridleway (Potter Lane) south, with open, hedgeless fields on both sides and a big sky overhead. Ignore the turning into Swalefields, continue south. Pass through Fairholme to Far Fairholme. M11,p40.

WP18
2.25 miles
SE to WP19
The tarmac stops and the path continues straight on through a gate, coming back to the levee on the edge of the river. It eventually turns away from the river again just after Rush Farm and joins another narrow lane (Pickeringmoor Lane) for the remaining distance into the village of Maunby. M12,p41.

WP19
0.3 miles
NE to WP20
Walk up the main street of Maunby, past the pub and to the corner at the top. Turn right, and then immediately left, towards South Otterington and Newby Wiske. M12,p41.

WP21
1.35 miles
NE to WP22
In Newby Wiske turn right and walk down hill to the bridge over the River Wiske, up the other side to arrive at the main road with the South Otterington Shorthorn directly opposite. M12,p41.

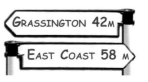

GRASSINGTON 42M

EAST COAST 58 M

Day Four

Terrain: Gently rising farmland before steady climb
onto the Cleveland Ridge
Distance: 15 miles
Total height gain 1640 ft
Highest point: 1215 ft
Constant walking time 5 hours
Allow 7 hours
Refreshments: Excellent pub at Knayton

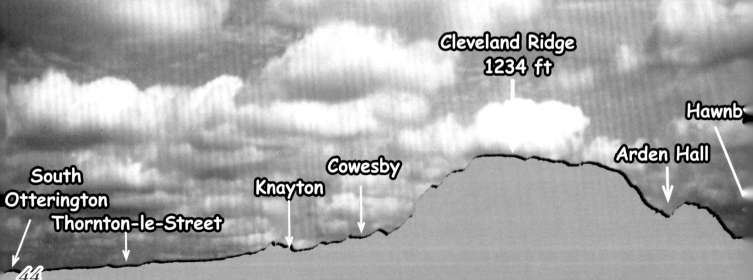

Cleveland Ridge
1234 ft

Hawnb

Arden Hall

South
Otterington
Thornton-le-Street

Knayton

Cowesby

South Otterington to Hawnby

This is a splendid day, interesting and a pleasure to the last step. It is the fourth day, the half way point is reached and the landscape changes. In a way, you could say it is up hill all the way from here!

It starts with a jolt! Walk towards Thornton-le-Moor and stop on the bridge which crosses the very fast north/south railway line. Wait for a train to come along and stand on the bridge above it. They come along every few minutes, so just wait for one and see what happens.

I think you will be impressed by the huge sweep of today's varied landscape. It is like a graceful curve. For a few more miles there is easy progress to be made which also gives time to warm up tired legs. Keep an eye on the soft and gentle terrain, because just before lunch at Knayton, there is a noticeable kick onto a little ridge. The Vale is running out and in a series of undulations it will bring you to the foot of the Cleveland Hills.

The Ridge has been visible from many viewpoints since the middle of the first day and now it is here. You are at the bottom of a steady climb that will test your legs. It is time to creak slightly and bend into the gradient. It is a short climb, perhaps a little too short, so when you have made the ridge cling to your prize for a mile north to enjoy the new views.

I hope there will be a clear view back to the line of Pennine Hills to the West, from whence we came and, of course, the reward for the climb, the view ahead. To the East there is a cascade of ridges and truncated hills that run north/south across our path and try to bar our progress. That is tomorrow's story, let it wait. Now, it is time to head down hill, down the slopes into the fray of a convoluted landscape to find the hidden valleys and dales of the North Yorkshire Moors - if you were expecting just moorland you will be so pleasantly surprised.

The Lane From Cowesby at the Foot of the Ridge

Day 4. South Otterington to Hawnby

WP01
1.7 miles
ENE to WP02

From South Otterington take the road to Thornton-le-Moor, crossing the Railway Bridge after a short half mile and following the road beyond Thornton-le-Moor to the A168. M13,p.48.

WP02
0.4 miles
NE to WP03

At the junction you will see a fingerpost at the gate just to the right, opposite, it points up the left hand side of the field and through another gate at the top. Ahead, through the next field, a farm comes into view, Crosby Grange, and the gate opens onto the farm track. M13,p.48.

WP03
0.5 miles
E to WP04

Don't follow the track but go through the gate straight opposite, on the inner corner of the bend, and into the field. Walk down to the bottom left hand corner. There was an electric fence on the left when I walked this way and there didn't appear to be a way out until

Map 13. South Otterington to Knayton Road

I saw a footbridge well concealed by an overgrown hedge. The next footbridge is easier to find and cross, with a third bridge over another small stream just beyond that. We are on the flats here and streams hang around, needing to be crossed. M13,p.48.

WP04
0.5 miles
E to WP05

Cross a stile into a field which has Broad Beck on the right, walk to the edge of the beck and follow it left for over half a mile, a pleasant beck full of life under the trees. The only problem is the newly constructed and ugly line of National Grid pylons that have been strung down the fields. What a pity they couldn't dig a hole and put the cables in it. The effect of the pylons is to put a new access road to one of the metal giants that is not marked on the map. When you climb into the new road, just before WP05, look for a continuation of the path across one small field before getting onto the proper road. M13,p.48.

WP05
0.75 miles
SE to WP06

Turn right and follow the road to Knayton, cross the busy A19 via the bridge. The pub is a hundred yards up the road on the left. M13/14,p.48/49.

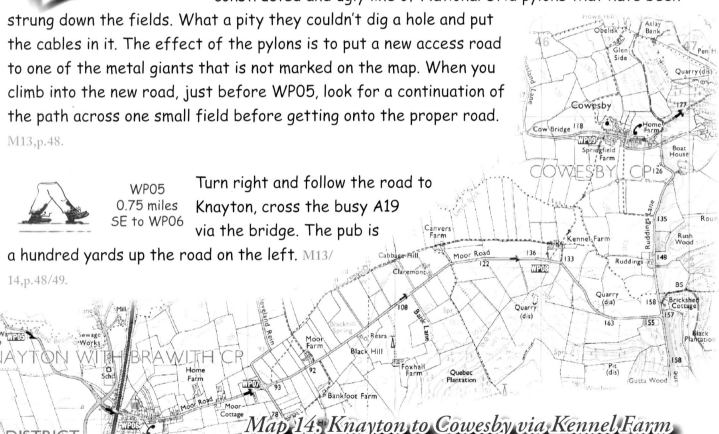

Map 14: Knayton to Cowesby via Kennel Farm

Lunch The Woof & Bang pub at Knayton is a sight for sore feet! It is open all day, every day, serving good food from a varied menu - BUT please take cash, Credit Card or Switch Card payments are not accepted, and you have to wash dishes for a week if you cannot pay!

WP06
0.5 miles
NE to WP07

After lunch, turn left along Moor Lane. At the crossroads walk straight on. Although there is a path between here and Cowesby it is so poorly marked and maintained that it has defeated my attempts to follow it. The lane to Kennel Farm, is easy on the feet and a pleasure to walk. M14,p.49.

WP07
1.25 miles
NE to WP08

Continue along Moor Lane as far as Kennel Farm. The fingerpost and stile is in the fence on the left as you draw level with the house. M14,p.49.

Getting steeper, onto the ridge above Cowesby

Arden Hall

WP08
0.5 miles
N to WP09

The path has been diverted and well marked. It now goes down the left hand side of a paddock and then round the left hand side of the house, to the back, through two more paddocks, and then strikes off towards Cowesby over a large field, north. M14,p.49.

WP09
0.6 miles
NE to WP10

Turn right on the road in Cowesby opposite the church. At the telephone box, the road jinks to the right but the route goes straight on up a back lane, it then turns to the left at Home Farm and at the fork turn right. It soon becomes a wonderful deep gully, lined and surrounded with trees, steep, and steady up onto the first ridge. M14,p.49.

WP10
0.75 miles
SE to WP11

On the first ridge (Pen Hill) turn right to follow the top edge of the trees with a wall, and then a track in a deep gully curling round Gallows Hill to a gate on the left. M14/15,p.49/52.

WP11
0.65 miles
NNE to WP12

Turn left through the gate. The path is a clear diagonal up the side of the hill - the last climb on to the Cleveland Ridge. M15,p.52.

WP12
0.95 miles
N to WP13

Turn left at the top and follow the ridge. You pass a gate on the left with tarmac road leading up to it. There is also a path on a right turn opposite the gate which follows an easterly spur which could be a good alternative if you are desperately tired or the weather is miserable but there is a better route on the right a few hundred yards further on. Keep to the ridge path, north. M15,p.52.

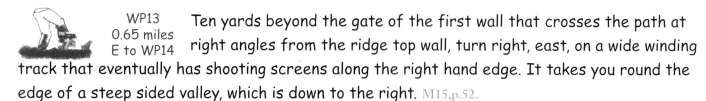

WP13
0.65 miles
E to WP14

Ten yards beyond the gate of the first wall that crosses the path at right angles from the ridge top wall, turn right, east, on a wide winding track that eventually has shooting screens along the right hand edge. It takes you round the edge of a steep sided valley, which is down to the right. M15,p.52.

WP014
0.5 miles
SE to WP15

Keep your height as the path turns south along the edge of Harker Yates Ridge, then there is a right hand fork and you can soon see below a tree filled valley with a small lake in it. M15,p.52.

WP015
0.25 miles
W to WP16

Turn sharp right down hill into the valley of Thorodale. M15,p.52.

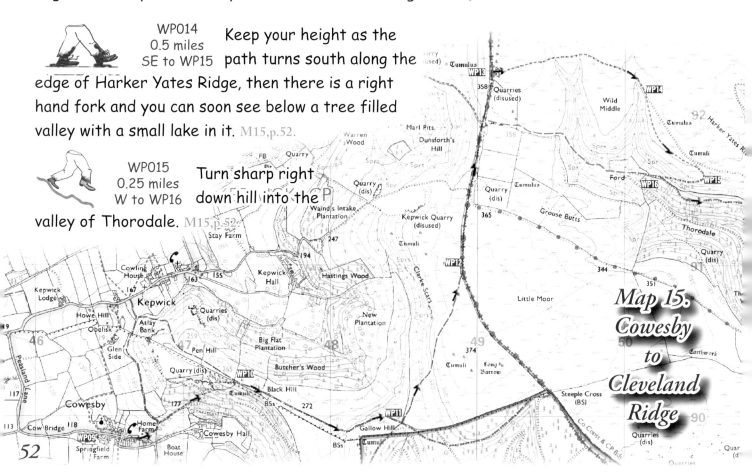

Map 15:
Cowesby
to
Cleveland
Ridge

WP16
1.25 miles
SE to WP17

Turn sharp left through the first gate at the top of the woods. The path remains fairly high on the hillside in the trees, gradually descending. There are no sharp turns off the woodland path until you arrive at Nun's Well which is not obvious, turn through a sharp right hand corner at huge mature trees. M15/16,p.52/53.

WP17
0.35 miles
S to WP18

Follow the right hand bend down hill in the trees then over a short rise into the farm yard that is next to Arden Hall. The Hall is not open to the public but that doesn't stop you admiring the wonderful hedge on the far side from a polite distance. Walk up to the main gate onto the road and turn left. M16,p.53.

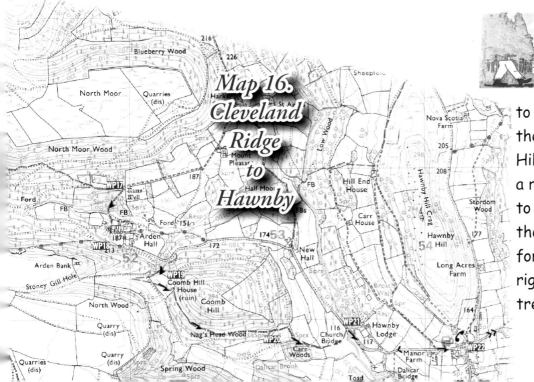

Map 16.
Cleveland
Ridge
to
Hawnby

WP18
0.5 mile
S to WP19

There is a track opposite the gate to Arden Hall that leads to the same place on Coombe Hill but it is not marked as a right of way. Walk down to the road and then at the left hand bend look for a footpath up a sharp right turn, back up into the trees. M16,p.53.

WP19
1 mile
SE to WP20

Beyond a five bar gate turn left in the field and walk over a mound (the remains of Coombe Hill House?) that obscures the view. Soon a yellow marker becomes visible and a gate into the thickly wooded path round Coombe Hill. The path follows the contour round the base of Coombe Hill through Nags Head Wood. You emerge onto the edge of the wood in a steeply descending field on the right. Don't go all the way round Coombe Hill or you will come out onto the road again (but if you do just turn right and follow the road). M16,p.53.

WP20
0.25 miles
E to WP21

Bear right down hill, through a gate and across another field to a stone bridge on to the road. M16,p.53.

WP21
0.5 miles
NE to WP22

At the stone bridge turn right and follow the road gently up hill to Hawnby. M16,p.53.

GRASSINGTON 57M

EAST COAST 43M

The View Back from the Cleveland Ridge

DAY FIVE

Terrain: Small green valleys, wooded glades, and streams. Low moorland and small plantations
Distance: 14 miles
Total Height Gain: 2200 ft
Highest point: 700 ft
Allow 7 hours
Refreshment: Nothing until Fadmoor

Hawnby

Rievaulx Moor

Shiplam Common

Birk Nab

Otterhills

Sleightholme Dale

Fadmoor

Hutton-le-Hole

Gillamoor

*I*f you summon
the strength that
you will need for this day's
walk by tensing muscles and stiff-
ening resolve, the chances are that you
will hurt yourself. Today's route is not a
back-breaking, lung tearing struggle, like
climbing through a mountain pass in a blizzard, but
it is over ground that seems to gently resist our easy
progress of the previous day. It is convoluted. It curls back on
itself and then reveals little hidden valleys, tree lined groves
harbouring secrets. It is a walk to be enjoyed, if time is taken to let the
day unfold, as your legs unfold the landscape.
Between the valleys and glades there are open moors with ridges running north

and
south.
And then a
final steady climb
through trees to a
plateau on the other side of
which is the village of Fadmoor.
When you are already reasonably
tired, the trick to staying happy, is to
avoid trying to do it in one giant stride. We
are not giants. We are little two legged animals
scurrying round in the undergrowth. If we keep to a
human pace there is no distance that cannot be walked
given enough time. Tell yourself to let the walk fill all the hours
of the day apart from those put aside to eat, drink, rest, talk, and
when the sun goes down sleep. The walk, with steady, measured steps,
with plenty of attention to the distant horizon, the sweep of the sky and of

course
the wandering
trail, will
eventually take care of
itself. You could run it,
heart almost bursting, sweat
pouring down your back, feet
burning with new formed blisters. But
what fun is that? Slow down here. It is a
fourteen mile day that should feel like a walk in
the park. This is an ancient landscape, different and
renewed every time the sun comes up, and you will be right
in the middle of it. A dot moving inexorably from 'A' to 'B', to
'C', and when you get to H it will be the wonderful village of
Hutton-le-Hole.

Bluebell Wood

Day 5. Hawnby to Hutton-le-Hole

WP01
0.20 miles
S to WP02

Walk down the hill from the Hawnby Hotel, to the corner before the bridge. M17,p.62.

WP02
0.75 miles
NE to WP03

Turn left into the field before Hawnby Bridge. Cross the flats to a footbridge and then turn half left up the hill with Ellers Wood on your right into hawthorn bushes and gnarled trees to find the stile onto the road. M17,p.62.

WP03
0.4 miles
NE to WP04

Turn right and follow the road to Wass House. M17,p.62.

WP04
0.3 miles
NE to WP05

Turn right down the hill across the fields to the top of the spur. M17,p.62.

WP05
0.25 miles
S to WP06

The path loops round south, off the spur to a footbridge at the meandering stream. M17,p.62.

WP06
0.4 miles
NE to WP07

Across the bridge, turn half left to enter the wood at a corner stile. In Feather Sike Wood (full of bluebells and the smell of wild garlic) the path leads through to the road at Feather Holme Farm. M17,p.62.

WP07
1 mile
NE to WP08

Turn left on the road and then immediately right into the next field and follow the path round with Low Wood on your left. M17,p.62.

WP08
0.4 miles
SE to WP09

Strike off half right across the field up the slope. At the edge of the wood turn left, with the wood covering Rievaulx Bank on your right and follow to a stile in the corner. M17,p.62.

WP09
1 mile
E to WP10

On the other side of the fence join a forest track that eventually crosse. the end of a tarmac road in the trees. Through Roppa Wood the trees open up on the left. M17/18,p.62/63.

WP10
0.75 miles
SE to WP11

The path then leaves the wide track for a much smaller woodland path. The track carries on to the left but the route continues straight on at the corner. The woodland path gradually turns towards the south and comes out of the trees at a road. M18,p.63.

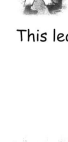

WP11
1 mile
NE to WP12

There is a telephone box up the road on the right and the path is a right turn next to it. This leads round to a field heading north-

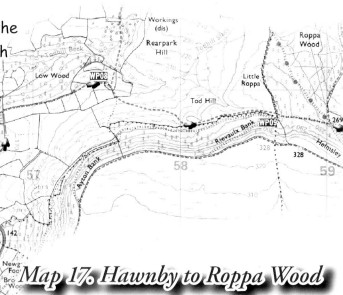

Map 17. Hawnby to Roppa Wood

east and you are accompanied by the howl of dogs that are in the grounds of the house on your left (don't worry, no more than ten people have been torn limb from limb by them). Head north-east past Lund Farm to a stream with the track going through it, turning more directly east as it does, then up the hill to Birk Nab Farm. M18,p.63.

WP12
0.3 miles
NE to WP13

Turn left in front of the house and then through the gate that is in front of you which leads into a huge open field. The path heads north and then turns abruptly south again. M18,p.63.

WP13
0.3 miles
E to WP14

So WP14 is only a couple of hundred yards directly east from here across the open field. M18,p.63.

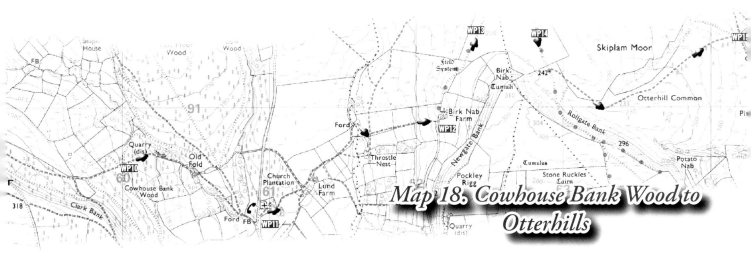

Map 18, Cowhouse Bank Wood to Otterhills

WP14
1 mile
E to WP15

Turn right (south) and look out for a narrow wood down the slope to your left – turn towards it and keep it on your right all the way down into the little valley with a beck running through it. M18,p.63.

WP15
1.25 miles
SE to WP16

Turn right and at Otterhills turn left and cross the bridge to turn right and follow the tarmac road up past Penny Holme to a sharp right hand corner. M19,p.64.

WP16
0.75 miles
SE to WP17

Follow the road round to the next farm house Aumery Park. M19,p.64.

WP17
0.35 miles
SE to WP18

A fingerpost on the left points off the road across the field and into the trees of Intake Plantation for a short steep climb. M19,p.64.

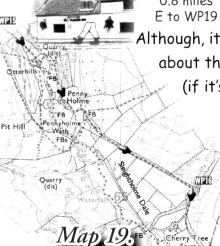

WP18
0.8 miles
E to WP19

Cross the fields, with clear well placed stiles to a back road, turn right and you arrive at Fadmoor, where there is a pub - The Plough. Although, it is probably well past lunchtime by the time you get here, there are about three more miles to Hutton-le-Hole, so a rest could possibly be endured (if it's open). M19,p.64.

Map 19:
Sleightholme Dale
to
Gillamoor

WP19
0.75 miles
NE to WP20

Turn left and follow the road to Gillamoor. Try **The Best Corner shop in the Universe'** on the left, for drinks & snacks. At the end of the village go down the right hand side of the church. M20,p.65.

WP20
0.7 miles
NE to WP21

Follow the lovely track round the back of the church and down the hill. At the bottom turn sharp right and continue to the Mill House. The path goes through the grounds on the left of the house and then crosses to a footbridge over the River Dove and into the field beyond. M20,p.65.

WP21
0.5 miles
NE to WP22

Just before Grouse Hall turn right into the field and head for the trees in the far corner where a footbridge leads to a track which you cross to follow a sheep trod onto the open moor. M20,p.65.

GRASSINGTON 72M

EAST COAST 28M

WP22
0.75 miles
NE to WP23

The path curls round the end of the ridge and joins a fenced path which leads to the road, turn right and Hutton-le-Hole is just round the corner. M20,p.65.

Day Six

Terrain: Country lanes and moorland, dense plantation and the 'Land That Time Forgot'
Plus a steam railway!
Distance: 13 miles
Total height gain: 1550 ft
Highest point: 845 ft
Constant walking time: 6 hours - allow 7
Refreshments: The ideally placed Hartoft Hotel

High Muffles
845 ft

Saltergate

Hutton le Hole

Levisham Station

Lastingham

Stepping Stones

Hutton-le-Hole to Saltergate

This is a great day's walk – savour it. There are three stages to this wonderful day. The first is an early detour to look at the crypt in the church at Lastingham. This guide has tried to emphasise the pleasure of a walk in the open air for seven whole days. So ten minutes among the stony, dusty relics of the past is an acceptable contrast to the vibrant colours of life outside don't forget to sign the visitors book - then let's get back outside.

This stage continues with similar terrain as yesterday - whaleback moors open to the north. Then, after lunch the change is quick and dramatic. An open track leads you into the huge and tightly planted Cropton Forest. Suddenly, the route delves into thick undergrowth and climbs steeply up into a wet jungle. The difficulties of the track do not last long but the skills of navigation and interpretation become more important when you try to keep your bearings and find a way out of here. There is a sameness to walking in woodland that is quite disorientating. It changes distances so you are not quite sure if it is three miles you have walked, or

four? The twists and turns of

the path need to be followed closely. When in

doubt trust the map rather than a linguistic analysis of my

waypoint descriptions - there is nothing more vague than clear instructions!

Don't worry, no-one has ever been permanently lost in these woods, at least, they have

always recovered a body.

Beyond Stape another change is due, a mile or two more of woodland and then suddenly the ground drops away and a deep snaking valley is at your feet. This is a valley with sheer cliffs, not rounded edges, and the meandering shape is also very familiar. It is a river valley where no river runs. Instead of a river, the valley is occupied by a railway, the historic Pickering line on which steam trains snake along the course of a long gone water way. It is the *Land That Time Forgot*, a valley carved by water that drained a huge glacial lake ten thousand years ago. As soon as the water had gone British Rail moved in, well, not quite straight away, they let the leaves dry out first in case they got on the line.

Day 6. Hutton-le-Hole to Saltergate

WP01
300 yards
SE to WP02

From the telephone box on the main street walk south to a stream with a footpath sign pointing left into the trees up Austin Head. M21,p.70.

WP02
1 mile
E to WP03

Climb the hill. The path levels out and heads east through fields to Spaunton. M21,p.70.

WP03
0.6 miles
E & S to WP04

Follow the road down into Lastingham, the Church on your left. M21,p.70.

WP04
1 mile
NE to WP05

Turn right in Lastingham and walk 150 yards to the junction. There is a footpath sign by a house to the right – this is the wrong one. Turn left and the footpath is 10 yards up on the right, it heads out of the village across low fields to the track below High Askew Farm. M21,p.70

Gorse along the road towards Lastingham

Turn left, almost north, and keep to this path looking out for stepping stones across the stream. Cross the stream and climb out onto the road next to a stone bridge.

WP05
1.25 miles
NNE to WP06

M21,p.70

Lunch

WP06
0.75 miles
to WP07 via
Hartoft

The route is to the right, but this is the last opportunity for a refresher and bite to eat, so if you could manage lunch turn left and walk 500 yards to the well appointed Hartoft Hotel. Then return to the bridge. 100 yards

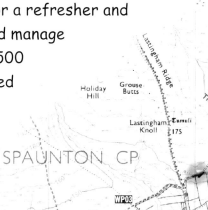

beyond is WP07.

M21,p.70

WP01
0.6 miles
NE to WP02

The alternative route to the same place for lunch is a bit more direct. It also starts from the telephone box in Hutton-le-Hole. Turn left up a ginnel and into gorse bushes to the road. M21,p70.

Map 21. Hutton-le-Hole to Cropton Forest

WP02
1 mile
NE to WP03

Turn right along the road towards Lastingham. After about half a mile, as the road turns to the right, leave it, to the left, onto the moor next to Mary Magdalene Well. This heads north but then turns NE towards Camomile Farm. M21,p70.

WP03
0.75 miles
NE to WP04

Continue onto the open moor. Drop down to the stream when the dip appears. M21,p70.

WP04
1.1 miles
NE to Stepping Stones (WP06)

Climb out the other side of the dip and continue in the same direction over Askew Rigg until you reach the stream. Follow it upstream until you find the stepping stones. (We waded across the stepping stones when they were about two inches under water - very refreshing). Onto the road at the stone bridge, left for lunch, right to continue the main route from WP07. M21,p70.

WP07
1 mile
NE to WP08

Turn left on to a wide forest track. Follow the track for a mile, then keep a look out for a yellow pointer on your right up into the trees. (See photo next page.)

WP08
2 miles
E to WP09

It is narrow and quite steep, dripping with water after rain and quite

Stepping Stones at Hartoft Bridge

difficult underfoot for the short but intrepid climb up into the huge Cropton Forest plantation. Cross two forest roads but continue up until it levels out where there is a cleared area, then follow the wide forest track heading east. Continue until you meet a junction and turn right, soon to arrive at a crossroads. M22,p.72.

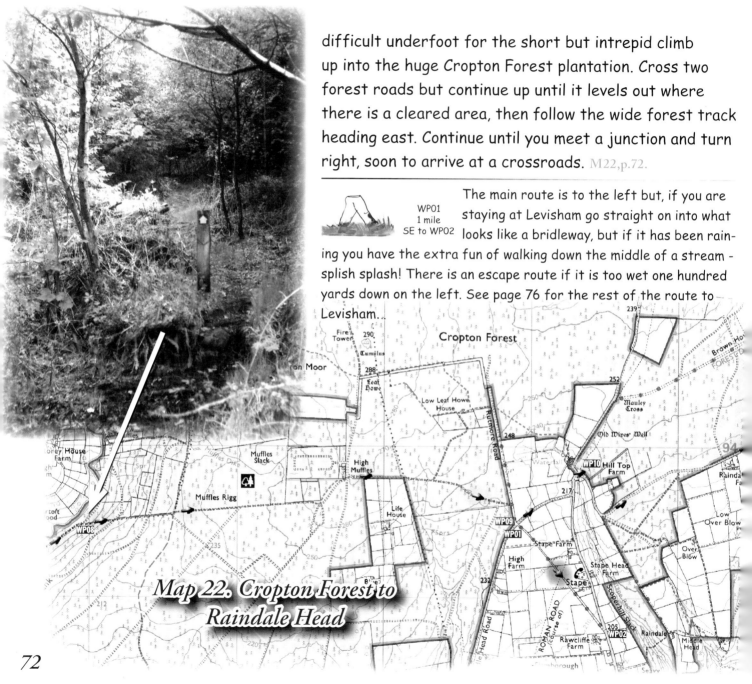

WP01
1 mile
SE to WP02

The main route is to the left but, if you are staying at Levisham go straight on into what looks like a bridleway, but if it has been raining you have the extra fun of walking down the middle of a stream - splish splash! There is an escape route if it is too wet one hundred yards down on the left. See page 76 for the rest of the route to Levisham.

Map 22. Cropton Forest to Raindale Head

WP09
0.35 miles
NE to WP10

The main route turns left for quarter of a mile, and then left again at the road junction, for a hundred yards, then takes the next right.

M22,p.72.

WP10
2.25 miles
NE to WP11

This road turns back on itself and heads almost south for a few hundred yards before turning left. It then continues north east through Raindale Head, with no turning apart from the bends of the track until the ground drops away and you can look down into an amazing valley.

M22/23,p.72/73.

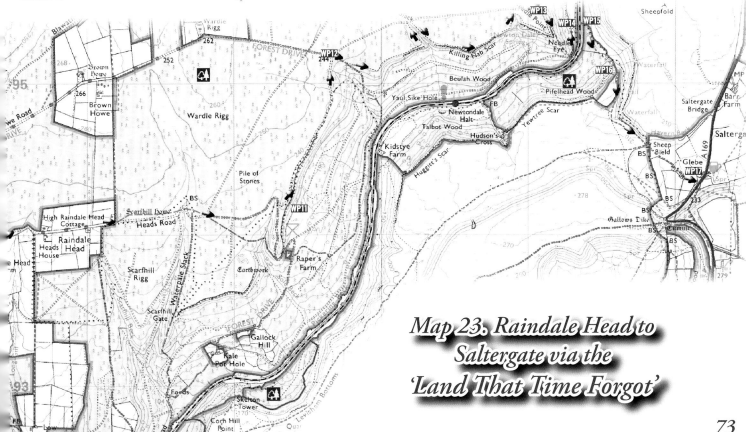

Map 23. Raindale Head to Saltergate via the 'Land That Time Forgot'

WP11
0.75 miles
N to WP12

Turn north with a spectacular cliff on your right, the track still wide enough for forestry vehicles (and Dinosaurs). M23,p.73.

WP12
1 mile
NE to WP13

At a sharp left-hand bend, a little path leads off to the right into the trees.Follow it and at the fork, 100 yards in, turn left, do not go down the hill signposted for Newtondale Halt. This wonderful cliff-top track follows the edge of a valley with spectacular views. At one point the path turns away from the cliff for a hundred yards, meets a forest road, turns right, then turns

Pickering's Train Set - chuff-chuff

right again and in a hundred yards it is back on the cliff top path again - Killing Nab Scar. Eventually the path turns away from the cliff a second time, follow it out to the forest road and turn right as far as the corner at Needle Point. M23,p.73.

WP13
0.6 miles
NE to WP14

At Needle Point, turn right under the trees, the path seems to peter out, but there is a bench there and the path heads steadily down the long spur, called Needles Eye, into the valley. At the bottom, turn left onto the forest track and walk out of the trees to a stile on the right. M23,p.73.

WP14
300 yards
NE to WP15

Cross two footbridges with stiles, one on each side of the railway line. This is a good place to have a break and wait for the next steam train to come along. M23,p.73.

WP15
0.25 miles
NE to WP16

When you resume, turn right and make for the steep end of the spur and climb the path that heads up it on the inner slope. If you are feeling intrepid follow the stream up the little valley on the left. There is a pleasant waterfall at the top which requires a bit of a scramble to get round. M23,p.73.

WP16
0.6 miles
SE to WP17

Follow the path out of the trees and over a couple of field to land in the car park of the Saltergate Hotel at WP17. M23,p.73.

Day 6. Alternative Route to Levisham.

The route to Levisham is a bit easier and there is more choice of accommodation but the route to Saltergate takes three miles off the last day's walk. If you do go to Saltergate you should still take a stroll in the evening down into the Hole of Horcum, it is a very impressive feature.

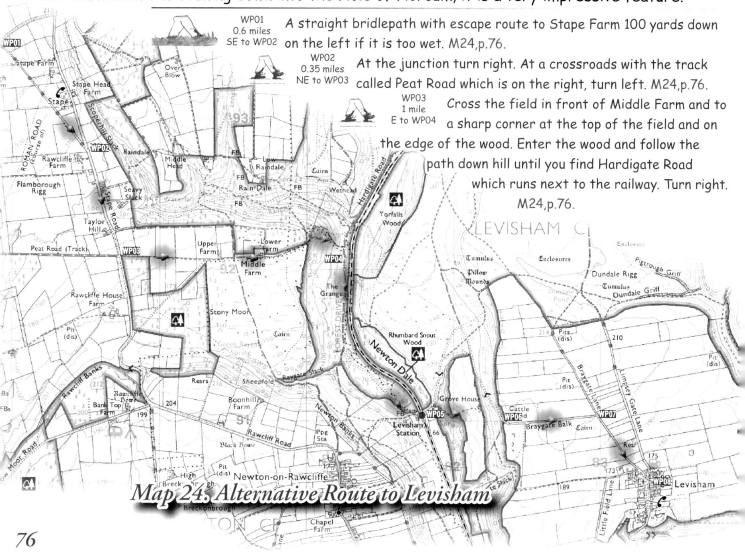

WP01
0.6 miles
SE to WP02

A straight bridlepath with escape route to Stape Farm 100 yards down on the left if it is too wet. M24,p.76.

WP02
0.35 miles
NE to WP03

At the junction turn right. At a crossroads with the track called Peat Road which is on the right, turn left. M24,p.76.

WP03
1 mile
E to WP04

Cross the field in front of Middle Farm and to a sharp corner at the top of the field and on the edge of the wood. Enter the wood and follow the path down hill until you find Hardigate Road which runs next to the railway. Turn right. M24,p.76.

Map 24. Alternative Route to Levisham

WP04
1 mile
S to WP05

Follow the wide track to Levisham Railway Station. M24,p.76.

WP05
0.75 miles
E & S to WP06

Cross the line & follow the road up hill then turn right into the trees. Climb though the trees steeply to Grove House then turn right, south, following the contour until a path on the left gives access to Braygate Balk. M24,p.76.

WP06
0.35 miles
E to WP07

Continue east to the next junction. M24,p.76.

WP07
0.35 miles
SE to WP08

Turn right and Levisham is ahead. M24,p.76.

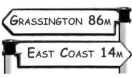

GRASSINGTON 86M

EAST COAST 14M

Through Cropton Forest

77

Day Seven

Terrain: Vast open moor before a gentle stroll
down to the sea
Distance: 14 miles from Saltergate
17 miles from Levisham
Constant walking time: 6 hours
Allow 8 hours.
Total Height gain: 700 ft
Highest point: 950 ft
Refreshment: Packed lunch

Levisham

Hole of
Horcum

Saltergate
Hotel

Malo Cross

Fylingdales
Moor

Lilla Cross

Jugger
Howe
Beck

Ravenscar

Robi
Hood
Bay

The last day of this walk is here. You have got this far so there is no way now that you can fail to complete it. Did it seem like that a couple of days ago? Perhaps it got a little difficult when the ground turned to waves that sucked the strength from your legs just at the moment when they were beginning to ache from the previous days' walks. Today's brilliant journey tests a different part of your strength - your remaining stamina. The walk across Fylingdales Moor requires several hours of steady, relaxed and well paced striding. Little legs across a big landscape, so big it seems to diminish our efforts to gain the other side, so that at times we appear to be standing still.

There is a false dawn to this day, if it is clear. When you are near Lilla Cross you will realise that the sky ahead has a distinct line across it and below that is the sea. To the south a headland can be seen with the unmistakable shape of Scarborough Castle, many miles away. Back west, are the higher, bleaker moors that we have avoided for the sake of some variety, and a few more trees. At this moment, do not relax too much, even as you descend off the moor into Jugger Howe Beck, the smell of the sea in the air, there is a steady five more miles to go, the last five miles can sometimes feel like the first ten.

The sky is now coastal, big with streaming clouds carried inland by the wind. The high moor here is a plateau so the horizon is truly massive, dizzying with the emptiness and lack of natural trees. Store it in memory for the evening, in the throng of people in Robin Hood's Bay, locals, and all the walkers from Wainwright's Coast to Coast, Cleveland Way walkers, and Lyke Wake Walk walkers. We congregate here, not as competitors but comrades to tell the tales of our journey, firmly planted on the earth, at the ground zero of our lives, every step, from there to here.

Robin Hood's Bay has become the centre of walking pilgrimage, the centre right on the edge of a great sea, a welcoming place that contrasts so strongly with the empty moor that had to be crossed to get here. Now is the time for comfort and human company, made warmer by the healthy glow on wind burned faces. There is no better solution to the problem of living a good life, using our time wisely, than to have spent a week fully occupied by an endeavour that will live in our minds for ever.

From Levisham: Day 7. Round or Through the Hole of Horcum to Saltergate

GRASSINGTON 85M

EAST COAST 18M

WP01
0.75 miles
N to WP02

Head out of Levisham up the road on the right at the top of the village, Limpsey Gate Lane, as far as Dundale Griff. M25,p.81.

WP02
2.5 miles
N to WP04

The most direct route to Saltergate is straight on over Levisham Moor keeping to the ridge with the Hole-of-Horcum on your right. M25,p.81.

WP02
0.5 miles
E to WP03

To walk through the Hole-of-Horcum, turn right into Dundale Griff.

2M5,p.81.

WP03
1.5 miles
NE to WP04

Turn left at the bottom and follow the track north, through a narrow tree-lined valley that eventually opens up into the amazing natural amphitheatre that is the Hole of Horcum. The 'Hole' is also known as the Devil's Punchbowl because it was apparently made when a giant scooped a handful

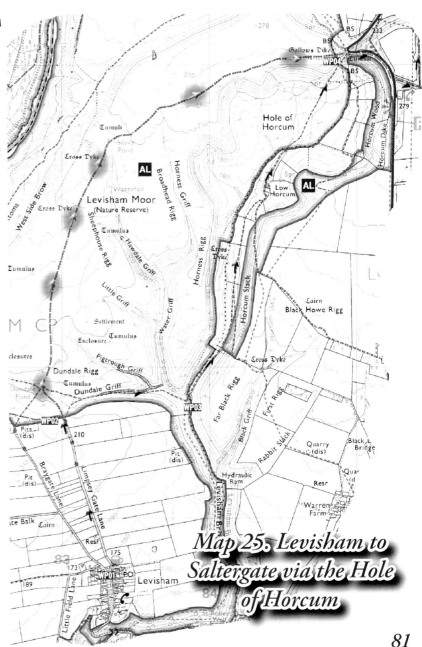

Map 25. Levisham to Saltergate via the Hole of Horcum

81

of earth out of the ground and threw it across the landscape at a rival. Some say it landed locally (Blakey Topping) but I've also heard that it landed near Market Weighton to become Arras Hill - that is 32 miles away! It could, of course, have been scooped out by a glacier. Ahead, you will see a derelict building, the path passes close by. Then it can be seen climbing steeply out to rejoin the other route at WP04. M25,p.81.

WP04
0.5 miles
E & N to Day 7 WP02

To join the main route from Saltergate you have a choice. You have only walked three miles of today's eighteen but this is the last opportunity for refreshments before heading off onto Fylingdales Moor. If you want a very early lunch turn left at the busy main road and walk down hill for 300 yards to the pub at Saltergate. Follow the directions from there on page 83.

To join up with Day 7 route without walking down to the pub turn right at the road until it levels out. A large car park can be seen on the other side of the road. Before you get to it a path turns into the trees for 150 yards east, then turns sharp left, behind the trees, north, for a quarter of a mile where it joins the main Day 7 route at WP02.

Down into Dundale Griff

The Hole of Horcum

ay 7. Saltergate to Robin Hood's Bay

WP01
0.2 miles
SE to WP02

Walk across the road from the Saltergate Hotel over the stile and up into the wood. The path goes right or left, turn left and climb up through the trees to the edge of the escarpment. M26,p.84.

WP02
1.1 miles
NE to WP03

The path follows the edge of the escarpment for half a mile before turning onto a gentle downward path on the left to Malo Cross, which stands next to the stile. M26,p.84.

WP03
1.3 miles
N to WP04

Turn left, over the stile and head north with the plantation on the right and the secret hush hush place showing through its invisibility screen on the left ahead. M26,p.84.

WP04
1.25 miles
E to WP05

At the northern tip of the plantation the path turns east again. Drop down into a short dip of Worm Sike Rigg and up the other side until the path curves back round north once more. M26,p.84.

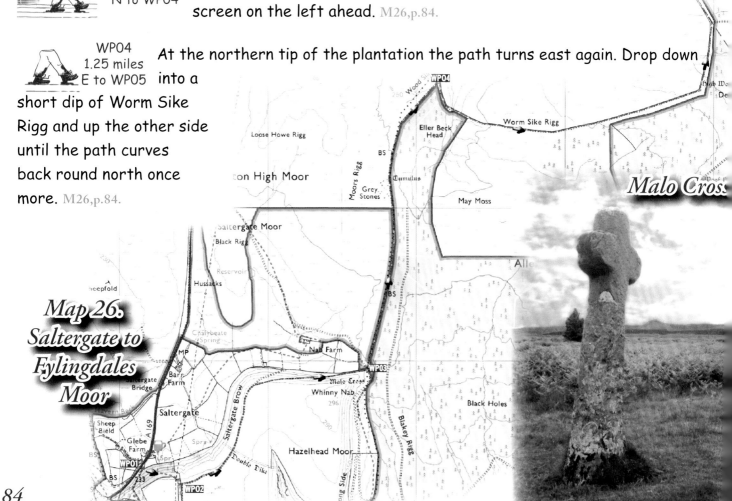

Map 26.
Saltergate to
Fylingdales
Moor

Malo Cross

WP05
0.85 miles
N to WP06

The plantation stops and there is open moor on both sides. On the skyline is the unmistakable cairn that surrounds Lilla Cross. M27,p.86.

WP06
2.75 miles
NE to WP07

From Lilla Cross follow the track that runs slightly north of east for over two miles through Burn Howe, (just a lump of stones on the moor) eventually dropping off the high moor into Jugger Howe Beck. M27,p.86.

WP07
1 mile
NE to WP08

Cross the rickety foot-bridge and head straight up the other side of the valley until you get to the road. M27,p.86.

WP08
2 miles
NE to WP09

Remain in the long lay-by which used to be an old corner of the Whitby – Scarborough Road long since remade. Turn right in the lay-by and

Lilla Cross

Fylingdales Moor

walk south to the bottom end, then cross the busy road to pick up the track in the heather. The path is broad and clear all the way to the coast above Ravenscar. Make for the transmitter mast - it is deceptively further than it looks. M28,p.87.

WP09
2.25 miles
NW to WP10

The pace has quickened. Tired legs have suddenly regained an extra spring. Below is the sea, and the welcome curve of Robin Hood's Bay. Turn

Map 27. Lilla Cross on Fylingdales Moor to Jugger Howe Beck

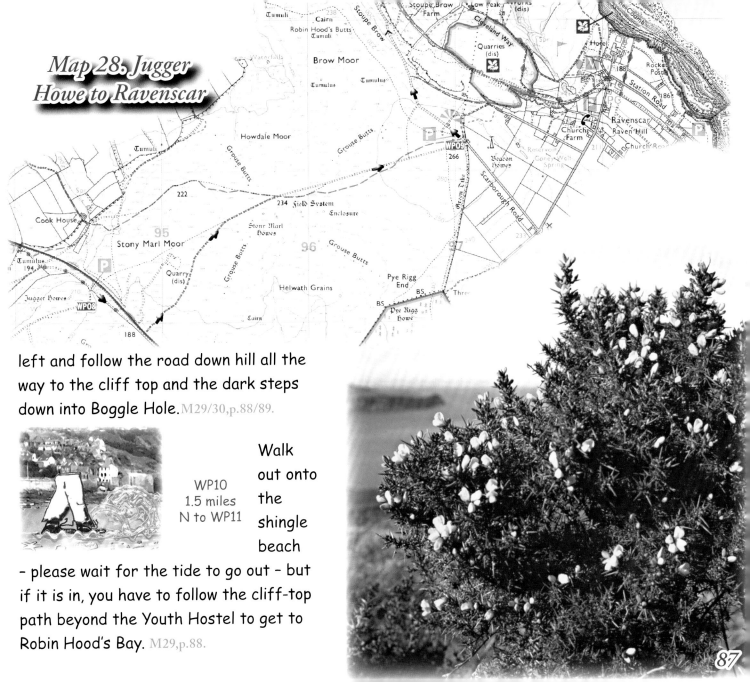

Map 28. Jugger Howe to Ravenscar

Tumuli
Cairn
Robin Hood's Butts
Tumuli
Stoupe Brow Farm
Low Peak Works (dis)
Cleveland Way
Quarries (dis)
Hotel
Colonel
Rocket Post
Station Road
186
188
Brow Moor
Tumulus
Tumulus
Ravenscar
Raven Hill
Church Farm
Church Road
Howdale Moor
Grouse Butts
Grouse Butts
266
Beacon Howes
Reservoir
Corey Well Spring
Tumuli
222
Cook House
234 Field System
Enclosure
Green Lane
Scarborough Road
231
Stony Marl Moor
95
Stony Marl Howes
96
Grouse Butts
97
Grouse Butts
Tumulus 194
Quarry (dis)
Helwath Grains
Pye Rigg End
BS
BS Three
Jugger Howes
210
WP08
188
Cairn
Pye Rigg Howe

left and follow the road down hill all the way to the cliff top and the dark steps down into Boggle Hole. M29/30,p.88/89.

WP10
1.5 miles
N to WP11

Walk out onto the shingle beach – please wait for the tide to go out – but if it is in, you have to follow the cliff-top path beyond the Youth Hostel to get to Robin Hood's Bay. M29,p.88.

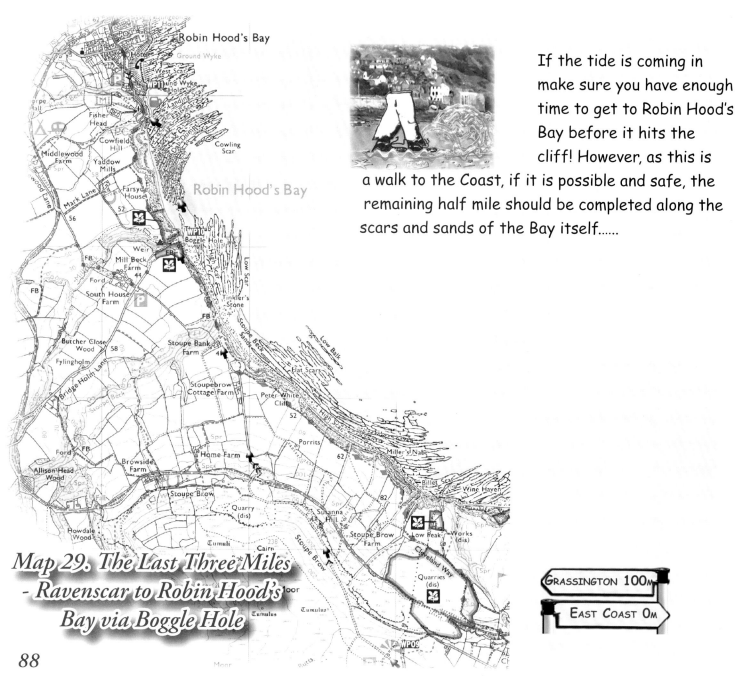

If the tide is coming in make sure you have enough time to get to Robin Hood's Bay before it hits the cliff! However, as this is a walk to the Coast, if it is possible and safe, the remaining half mile should be completed along the scars and sands of the Bay itself......

Map 29. The Last Three Miles - Ravenscar to Robin Hood's Bay via Boggle Hole

GRASSINGTON 100M

EAST COAST 0M

....and so to the sea.

Robin Hood's Bay

*Views of
Robin
Hood's Bay*

THE BAY HOTEL

Day 1.

Day 2.

Day 3.

Day 4.

Day 5.

Day 6.

Day 7.

If you encounter any serious difficulty follow the directions in this guide, please make a note and send a copy of this page to the author: John White, c/o Fractal Press, 1 Low Mill Cottages, Grassington. BD23 5BX.

PREPARATION

Although this is not the hardest walk to complete, 100 miles of open country is always going to demand plenty of effort and preparation. Blisters are second only to toothache for discomfort so they are best avoided at all costs. There are some special blister pads on the market that do an excellent job, and these should be used even if a blister has not yet formed but when you are experiencing a sore point. Of course, buying a new pair of boots the day before you start the walk - or setting off in a pair of size twelve wellington boots! - is not the best plan. With boots that are properly worn-in (at least 100 miles of previous walking) and good socks, your feet should remain happy and the whole week will be a pleasure. With regard to socks, the inner pair could be what are called 1000 mile socks. They are a double sock that reduces the risk of blisters because the outer layer moves against the inner rather than against your skin. The more modern wickable thick socks are very comfortable, especially when new. I would recommend taking five or six brand new pairs of the thicker outer socks so that you have a spongy cushion to walk on for most of the day. They do compact quite quickly, and remain compacted until the next wash. Also, take your boots off at lunch time to give your feet a rest, and consider changing socks, there is nothing better than a nice cool pair of socks to refresh hot feet (apart from a paddle in a freezing cold stream).

Another source of misery is running out of energy. If the walk is more demanding than your normal daily routine you have to eat more food than you usually do. You will not put on weight, that is virtually impossible with the energy you will burn along the way. You must stoke the engine to keep up with the demands you are placing on yourself. This can be accomplished with the greatest of pleasure and in a way that adds to the general enjoyment of each day - LUNCH. Even if you are not very hungry you should eat lunch. The food you eat at lunchtime on day one is what you will burn during day two. Most of the pubs and cafes mentioned in the guide do very good lunches that provide high energy meals and special high energy athletes beer! It is something to look forward to each day, sitting in a pub or cafe for an hour or so, having a rest, good conversation and good food.

With regards to carrying things the greatest pleasure comes from the lightest load. One of the best savings in money and weight is this guide book, you will not need to buy, or carry, the four maps you would otherwise need to complete the walk, everything is here between these pages.

The other things you need are so obvious I'm not going to list what you already know.

With regards to GPS, at some stage there will be a complete list of the waypoints of the route that will be available for download from the website at fractalpress.co.uk. You will need a Garmin GPS and computer to use the information.

ACCOMMODATION

Grassington:

The Foresters Arms, 20 Main Street, Grassington, Nr Skipton, North Yorkshire BD23 5AA 01756 752349

Devonshire Arms, Grassington Square, Grassington. 01756 752 525

Mayfield B&B, Suzanne Trewartha, Mayfield, Low Mill Lane, Grassington, N.Yorks, BD23 5BX. 01756 753052
suzanne@mayfieldgrassington.co.uk

Kirkfield B&B, Hebden Road, Grassington. BD23 5LJ 01756 - 752 385

Nidderdale:

Crown Hotel, Middlesmoor, Pateley Bridge, Harrogate,North Yorkshire, HG3 5ST. Tel: 01423 755204

The Crown at Lofthouse, Lofthouse, Tel: 01423 755206

Snape:

Castle Arms Inn, Snape, Near Bedale, North Yorkshire, DL8 2TB
Telephone: 01677 470270
Fax: 01677 470837. castlearms@aol.com

South Otterington

Otterington Shorthorn Pub, 01609 773816

Hawnby
The Hawnby Hotel

Hawnby, Nr. Helmsley, N. Yorks, YO62 5QS
Telephone 01439-798202 info@hawnbyhotel.co.uk
Easterside Farm, Hawnby, Hemsley, YO62 5QT. Tel: 01439 798277
email: sarah@eastersidefarm.co.uk

Laskill Grange, Nr Hawnby, Helmsley, North Yorkshire, YO62 5NB Mrs Sue Smith: Tel 01439 798268 Email:
j.fairburn@farmline.com

Hutton le Hole

Mrs J Fairhurst, Barn Hotel and Tearoom, Hutton le Hole, North Yorkshire, YO62 6UA, Tel: 01751 417311.
Email: fairhurst@lineone.net
Moorlands of Hutton-le-Hole, North Yorkshire Moors, York YO62 6UA,
Tel: 01751 417 548, Fax: 01751 417 760,
Email: info@moorlandshouse.co.uk
There are plenty of other options for accommodation on the weblink below:
http://www.yorkshire-tour.co.uk/hutton.htm

Lastingham:

only a couple of miles further if you would like to stay in an unspoiled pub
The Blacksmith's Arms 01751 417247

Levisham

Moorlands Hotel, Levisham, Nr Pickering, North Yorkshire, YO18 7NL
Telephone: 01751 460229 Fax: 01751 460470
The Horseshoe Inn, Main Street, Levisham, Pickering, YO18 7NL
Tel: 01751 460240 Fax: 01751 460240
Email: info@horseshoeinn-levisham.co.uk

Saltergate

The Saltergate Inn
Saltergate, North Yorkshire. Tel: 01751 460237

Robin Hood's Bay

The Victoria Hotel, Station Road, Robin Hoods Bay, N Yorks YO22 4RL
Tel: 01947 880205, Fax: 01947 881170
The Bay Hotel, The Dock, Robin Hood's Bay
Whitby North Yorkshire. YO22 4SJ. Tel: 01947 880278

There are camp grounds at all the evening stops along the route if you prefer camping.

BIOGRAPH by John White

If you would like something completely different to read at the end of each day of this walk, why not try *Biograph* by John White. It is a Science Fiction story set in the 22nd century, partly based in Yorkshire, USA & the space between here and the moon. And it doesn't stop there. If you ever wondered what the internet might have evolved into in 150 years time, this could be it! ISBN: 1870735153 £7.99.

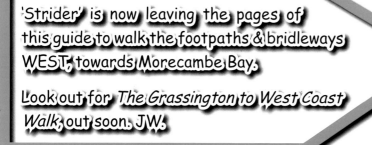

'Strider' is now leaving the pages of this guide to walk the footpaths & bridleways WEST, towards Morecambe Bay.

Look out for *The Grassington to West Coast Walk*, out soon. JW.